"By having the different ki   igh-lighted in this book you wi   dn't help but think that all marriages should begin with these sort of conversations, not just those bound for prenups."

—*Leisa Peterson*
Life and Money Coach for Entrepreneurs

"As a wealth psychologist, I know that many couples are searching for just such a resource to help guide them on how to broach the prenup conversation in a way that is trust building as opposed to trust eroding. Emily Bouchard and Emily Chase-Smith have provided just such a resource in this easy to read and apply guide."

—*Dr. Jamie Traeger-Muney*
Founding Principal, Wealth Legacy Group

"A must read for anyone contemplating a 2nd marriage (or 1st or 3rd...) With so many of my generation looking at 2nd (and 3rd) marriages or marriage-like commitments, this book couldn't have come out at a better time or with better information."

—*Jill Davis*
Master Coach, Speaker and Author

"Here's the big message: It's not about the money or protecting yourself. It's about setting up a marriage for success. This is a radical reframe on a prenup as a way to affirm and grow your relationship through a conscious exploration of values."

—*Steve Levin, Executive Coach and Founder*
of Powerful Conversations training

"This beginners' guide to prenuptial agreements takes the terror out of the idea of prenups by returning the power and responsibility to the couple themselves, beginning with the simple fact that everyone who marries gets a prenup, like it or not. That's because the laws of your state will govern what happens to the money if you divorce, and so it's smart to think about whether that would work well for you or whether you'd rather craft something more customized for your own values and circumstances. The authors guide readers through straightforward principles for having constructive conversations about money values and needs. Any couple contemplating marriage will have a stronger foundation for success after reading this book, whether they decide to create their own agreement or not."

—*Pauline H. Tesler, Esq.*
Director, Integrative Law Institute at Commonweal

"This is an amazing book, written in a way that keeps the reader engaged through the many thoughtful tips and exercises, all geared toward helping the soon-to-be- married couple navigate the challenging process of creating a prenuptial agreement. Bouchard and Smith help couples envision a very different process that produces more than the usual obligatory legal agreement by offering instead a vision that gives them the a way to use this process to strengthen their relationship."

—*Nancy Ross, LCSW, BCD*
Divorce Coach, Mediator, Trainer, Psychotherapist,
and Communication Specialist for Trusts and Estates

Beginners Guide to Purposeful Prenups

Beginners Guide to Purposeful Prenups

Three Essential Elements for a Successful Prenup Conversation

Emily Bouchard, MSSW & Emily Chase Smith, Esq.

For information, please contact:
purposefulprenups.com
336 Bon Air Center, #145
Greenbrae, CA 94904

ISBN eBook: 978-0-9975242-8-4
ISBN Paperback: 978-1-947341-15-9

Interior Design: Ghislain Viau

Foreword

For the last nearly twenty years, I've worked with hundreds of couples who want to create, or revise, their estate plans. Trust me, we've talked about almost everything you can imagine while doing so—the quiet joy of parents reviewing a long life well lived, worries about children who fail to thrive, secret children, and even Zoroastrian air burial traditions.

But there's one conversation that many of my clients have found really hard--talking about money within the context of their marriage, and especially sorting out what property is shared and what is separate.

I so wish that I could have given all of my clients this book, and that they'd read it. The Emilys (Bouchard and Chase Smith) nail it—they understand that the topic of money within a relationship is hard because it touches on so much more than dollars and cents.

Talking about money within a relationship opens us up, just as talking about death does, to our most deeply held values and our most deeply felt fears. And because of that, many of us just try and avoid both conversations. I can't tell you how many times I've worked with couples who had been married for many years, but had never, even once, broached the subject of how their property was owned.

But, of course, avoidance can only last so long. For those who need to discuss the topic of money within a relationship, this book is a great place to start. It is so much more than a dry, technical description of what a pre-nup is or a fear-based rationale for creating one. Instead, you'll find tools to help the conversation begin, and ways to keep the conversation respectful, loving, and even surprisingly revealing and intimate.

After all, *how* we talk to each other about money (and let's face it nearly everything else) is just as important as *what* we talk about. Here, the Emilys actually take their own advice. Their book, like their recommendations for a prenup conversation, is meaningful and effective because they:

1. Keep it specific and present.
2. Keep it short and to the point.
3. Keep it personal and meaningful.

Enjoy!

Liza Hanks, Esq., Partner GCA, LLP, Certified Specialist in Estate Planning, Trust Administration & Probate Law, author of *Estate Planning for Busy Families* and *The Trustee's Legal Companion*, both published by Nolo. Her third, *Every Californian's Guide to Estate Planning*, is due out January of 2018.

Introduction

"T'ain't what you do, it's the way that you do it."
—Melvin "Sy" Oliver and James "Trummy" Young

Congratulations! You're engaged! A wedding, marriage, and life together are exciting, but the prenup, not so much. Maybe you've put off the prenup conversation as long as you can, but the wedding date is getting closer and you know you need to broach the subject before it's too late. Maybe you've attempted to talk about a prenup a few times and it hasn't gone well so you're looking for a new approach. Or, maybe your fiancé has brought up the reality that the two of you need to discuss a prenup and you're looking for resources to help you understand what this means and why you need one. Wherever you are in the process, know that like almost everyone else who reaches this place:

1.   This is probably NOT what you want to be thinking about right now.
2.   You're experiencing all kinds of emotions about this, from anxiety to dread.
3.   You want your marriage to be solid and strong, and you don't want to do damage to it just as it's getting started.

Prenups and prenup conversations can be intense and emotionally charged and for these reasons have gained a bad reputation. The hit show "Seinfeld" demonstrated the pervasive view of prenups in one of their memorable episodes when George got cold feet after getting engaged to Susan. He flew into a panic and asked his friends how to get out of the wedding.

"You really want to get out of this thing?" asked Kramer. "I got two words for you: 'pre . . . nup'."

Elaine chimes in: "I wouldn't sign one."

This bit of comedy is based on the kernel of truth that even bringing up the concept of a prenup tanks a relationship. With this floating in the background, who wouldn't be at least a little nervous to have the conversation? Kanye West's 2005 smash hit "Gold Digger" created a wave of homemade videos of people singing "Gotta get a prenup!" A mashup of a scene from Seinfeld with Kanye's "Gold Digger" lyrics shows our love/hate relationship with prenups remains alive and well.

What to Expect from This Book

This book is very different from other publications about prenups because it focuses foremost on who the two of you want to be with each other as you approach the subject. Reading this book will help you begin to understand what impacts our ability to talk about money openly, and will give you some approaches to use right away as you begin to discuss your prenup. We wrote this book not from a legal perspective, but rather, a relational one. While we do provide guidance in the legal department, the focus of this book is primarily on how to keep your relationship strong as you cross the prenup bridge.

When it's your turn to cross the bridge, all the advice focused on "why" a prenup is so important, "what" a prenup is, and "what" you need to be sure to cover in your prenup, is relatively useless if you don't know HOW to have the conversation—arguably the most important part. The majority of articles and books barely touch the relational side. The few that do broach the relationship or communication side of the equation give the advice to "talk openly" about money with your partner/fiancé—the classic "easier said than done." Definitely "have an open conversation . . ." and while you're at it, go ahead and lift this 250-pound weight over your head!

So, let's get started with some of the heavy lifting, with the goal of having the whole experience feel lighter and easier as you go...

Prenups 101

*"A great marriage is not when the 'perfect couple'
comes together. It is when an imperfect couple learns
to enjoy their differences."*
—Dave Meurer

Before discovering how to talk about prenups, we want
to give you easy-to-understand information about what
prenups are and what they are not. We also debunk two
common misconceptions about prenups and give some
useful statistics about prenups.

So, What Exactly Is a Prenup?

According to Black's Legal Dictionary, a prenuptial
agreement is:

*A written contract between two people who are about
to marry, setting out the terms of possession of assets,*

treatment of future earnings, control of the property of each, and potential division if the marriage is later dissolved. These agreements are fairly common if either or both parties have substantial assets, children from a prior marriage, potential inheritances, high incomes, or have been "taken" by a prior spouse.

LegalZoom, a site that supports people in navigating legal matters, explains prenuptial agreements this way:

A prenuptial agreement is entered into before marriage. This agreement can set forth what will happen to your and your spouse's assets and income in the unfortunate event of divorce, separation, or death. Most importantly, a prenuptial agreement can preserve the nature of property in the event the marriage ends. In other words, separate property can remain separate instead of being subject to community property or equitable distribution laws.

(Note: Those of you who are living together and don't intend to get married, but still want the benefits of a prenuptial agreement can enter into a cohabitation agreement, which covers the same areas. And for those of you who are already married, you can draw up a document called a post-nuptial agreement.)

The prenup conversation can begin in many ways: you may bring it up, your future spouse may bring it up, or the conversation may originate from your parents or grandparents, or even your family's legal or financial advisor. No matter how it originates, *we believe every couple should have a prenup conversation as a way to strengthen your marriage* and bring you closer together as you discover how to navigate stressful, difficult, embarrassing, challenging topics with ease, grace, respect and love—especially in the area of money.

Research tells us that money is most often cited as the predominant reason for conflict in relationships and is the number one cause of divorce—*the number one cause!*[1] To be clear, money is neutral; it is not the cause of anything. **It is our inability to have healthy, relationship-affirming conversations with each other about money that creates ongoing conflict and dissatisfaction.** When you have the prenup conversation before marriage, you are creating healthy patterns around money, which help you build a foundation that will serve you for your entire marriage.

Two Prenup Misconceptions

As we begin, let's start with two often-overlooked premises in the world of prenups. The **first**, whether you like it or not, is that there is no "happily ever after" when it comes to marriage. Even the most loving and satisfying marriage ends—due to death, disability, divorce, or disinterest. This can sound pessimistic and morbid, but when you embrace the truth that every marriage ends, you realize your prenup planning is not only for divorce; it's for the end of a relationship, however that may occur. The **second** misconception is that you don't need a prenup since you know you are not going to divorce. Since a prenup covers way more than divorce, it helps you articulate and plan for all possible outcomes at the end of your marriage.

Here's one more that isn't a misconception, but rather a misunderstanding. Many people fail to realize that the moment you get married, **you already have a prenup**. How your finances will be divvied up has already been established by the lawmakers in your state through the codes that cover family law and estate planning. If you never have a prenup conversation, they'll step in and make all the decisions. You already have a prenup, one that you have absolutely no say in, so there's no point in getting defensive about the topic at all. Taking on this conversation will empower you to make your own choices and make joint decisions what matters to you right from the get-go.

Prenup Stats

For those of you who can't get enough of facts, here are a few data points about divorce, marriage, money and prenups:

- 15% of people who have been through a divorce regret not having a prenuptial agreement in place[2]
- There's been a fivefold increase in prenuptial agreements over the past 20 years
- The "great wealth transfer" of assets from baby boomers and their beneficiaries is expected to exceed $30

trillion over the next few decades—that will precipitate more than a few prenups.[3]

- The three top reasons for a prenup are protection of separate property, alimony/spousal maintenance, and the division of property.
- Steven Spielberg settled for $100 million after a prenup on a napkin was considered invalid.[4]
- Only 5% of divorces that occur in the United States have a prenup.[5]

These statistics further highlight that getting on the same page about money at the beginning of marriage is of ultimate importance. Why then is it so difficult?

Building a Solid Foundation

This book is written by two Emilys, Emily Bouchard and Emily Chase Smith. We have different backgrounds and different motivations, but share a desire to help couples begin their marriage from a place of strength.

Over the last fifteen-plus years, Emily Bouchard and the team at Wealth Legacy Group, have worked with hundreds of couples looking to heal the damage caused by unaddressed hurt and resentment related to their finances. For many of them, those hurts began to take root during their prenup negotiations. Addressing pain like that from the past is hard work. It can be expensive and intense, and takes intentional, consistent effort over time. Both members of the couple need to be willing and committed to shifting long-standing patterns of relating that have created a great deal of frustration and dissatisfaction in their marriage.

During the coaching process Wealth Legacy Group clients learn how to build new skills and how to bring healthy new approaches to their relating about money. Over time they are able to slowly and steadily change their trajectory. Bouchard became passionate to look for **ways to prevent those hurts from happening in the first place** and began developing the Purposeful Prenups process back in 2012 while writing *Estate Planning for the Blended Family* with L. Paul Hood, Jr. Writing this book, and the more in-depth *Purposeful Prenups* book is a labor of love for Bouchard, who hopes to provide an avenue for greater ease of relating between couples and their advisors around important financial and estate planning decisions, while bringing greater peace and connection to couples who want their love and marriage to go the distance.

One of the biggest motivators for Emily Chase Smith, a successful entrepreneur, author and attorney, to co-author this book and the larger book *Purposeful Prenups* is to train lawyers and therapists in this process. She's a single mother with three children and should she remarry, she will want both a prenup and a strong marriage. Chase Smith wanted to write the book SHE wanted to read and use in order to have the strongest future marriage possible.

We figured that if we both wanted this book for ourselves, there's a good chance other women would want it too. Our aim is to give you a foundation that is firm and strong enough to be able to withstand the myriad of challenges you will inevitably face together in your marriage. **We want your union to be rock-solid so that you know, no matter what, you've got what it takes to stay connected, stay committed, and stay in love.** That's what we want for ourselves too. We believe that knowing HOW to have your prenup conversation will greatly increase your chances for a successful, fulfilling, and happy marriage for the rest of your life.

Avoiding Cracks in Your Foundation

"Contempt is the sulfuric acid of love."
—John Gottman[6]

When building a new home, the most important, and often the most labor-intensive part of the process is pouring the foundation upon which the house will stand for years to come. Imagine for a moment that when you got engaged, you began to mix and pour the cement that will be the foundation of your marriage. The cement mixture needs to have the right blend of ingredients to allow it to be smooth, have the right consistency, and harden completely and evenly so that it can last a long time, no matter what earth-shattering events you both encounter.

Now imagine that as your relationship's foundational cement is poured, leveled and beginning to set, you have your prenup conversation. It starts out well enough, but some things are said that are hurtful or confusing. You each become defensive and begin to do what anyone who is feeling attacked does: defend yourself by attack back. Perhaps this takes place in subtle passive-aggressive ways: a sarcastic comment, a hurtful look, or the ever popular "whatever," or perhaps in more direct ways, by pointing out flaws, debts, or poor choices. Every time you go the route of hurting one another, you begin to plant seeds of resentment, resignation, and regret into your wet cement.

Over time, those painful seeds take root and cause cracks in your foundation. You trip over them every time you have a conversation about money in your marriage. Each time money talk begins, the same complaints arise, the same attacks occur, the same emotions emerge, all of which fertilize those roots to grow even deeper and make the cracks wider.

In an attempt to keep further damage from occurring, one or both of you will likely end up resorting to the seemingly logical, but highly detrimental, choice of avoiding money conversations altogether. Avoidance can be a useful short-term tactic, but, as marriage researcher John Gottman, who can predict with over 90 percent accuracy if a couple will stay married or not, discovered after researching over three thousand couples, how you avoid and to what degree, can have long-term consequences leading to your marriage ending and you both being thoroughly dissatisfied. The avoidance tactics that do the most damage are "stonewalling" and "emotional disengagement".[7]

Gottman's research, outlined in his groundbreaking book *The Seven Principles for Making Marriage Work*, reveals that avoidance, or "stonewalling," happens when the first three adaptive strategies of criticism, defensiveness, and contempt don't work and conflict continues. The resulting stonewalling gives you no one to relate to at all and can create major problems in your relationship and with your finances. You have serious issues to address, but you cannot talk to each other.

You can see how obvious it is that these behaviors, if left unchecked, all fertilize those initial seeds of hurt and resentment planted in your foundation, and create deep cracks that are hard to mend. We are committed to showing you how to talk about money in ways that shore up your foundation and give you a great future.

Three Essential Ingredients to Building a Solid Foundation

"When there is trust, conflict becomes nothing but the pursuit of truth, an attempt to find the best possible answer."
—Patrick Lencioni

When you think about getting started with the prenup conversation, you will most likely be thinking about the CONTENT of the conversation—who gets what? Who will own what? What's mine? What's yours? What's ours?

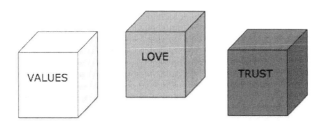

We suggest that you will be much more successful by starting out with the CONTEXT of the conversation—Why are we together? Why is it important to talk about this? How do we each think and feel about money? What are the things we value the most about each other and our future life together? In what ways to do we know we can count on each other and trust each other?

The foremost ingredients to having a strong, firm, solid foundation as you speak about your future, and your needs and wants related to financial support, are the building blocks of **Core Values, Loving Acknowledgments, and Authentic Trust**.

What follows is our attempt to give you immediate support and resources to assist you in connecting on these three levels, and to assist you in building your foundation in a way that will withstand the test of time.

1. Core Values: Clarify your Shared Values Regarding Money, Family, and the Future

"Each additional day together is a gift. The end of the day means the end of hostilities, the recognition that the underlying shared values and commitment to the relationship trump the need for one last dig or self-righteous justification."
—Daniel Kahneman

Since you're engaged and planning to get married, chances are you've already had a number of conversations about

what matters most to each of you when it comes to family, raising children, work/life balance, health and well-being, education, politics, religion, and more. You've also had plenty of time to observe each other and how you express those values in your actions, not just in your words. One of the most obvious ways we can discover our actual values when it comes to money is in how we each spend, save, invest, and give.

A great place to start the prenup conversation is by sharing with each other your particular memories and stories about money in your respective childhoods. We take in money messages from very young ages, and our values and approaches to money are well established by the time we are seven years old.[8] By sharing with each other your earliest memories about money, you begin to build trust with your partner regarding financial discussions. This can be tender and vulnerable, and can also be exciting and uplifting, or there may be shame, embarrassment, and/or guilt involved. For instance, people don't realize that almost EVERYONE has a story from his or her childhood about taking money and getting caught. How that painful lesson was handled by the adults at the time had an impact, and you will learn about the meaning each of you internalized about money when that happened in your life. Sharing memories like that one will help to build a foundation of understanding about how experiences shaped what each of you thinks and feels about money and relationships.

One way to make this experience positive is to have a goal in mind and an activity to do together. For instance, as you share money memories and messages with each other, you can capture them on sticky notes or index cards. These can be phrases often quoted by a parent or relative, or they can be the meaning you took away from memorable events, such as those that involved a purchase or a gift. Ideally, use two different colors, so you can tell whose responses are whose.

For instance, Emily B. has a vivid memory from when she was four or five years old. She recalls getting up the courage to ask her father if she could have a "clown cone" when they went to Baskin-Robbins for ice cream. She remembers her surprise and delight when he said yes. (*Meaning revealed:*

Asking for what you want is risky and can be disappointing, so you need to gear up). After paying for their ice cream, they went out of the store and she took her first lick and *plop*, the clown-faced ball of ice cream fell to the sidewalk. She recalls looking down at it, looking up at her father, and knowing she (1) couldn't cry, and (2) couldn't ask for another one. (*Meaning revealed: By that young age she already knew "Don't cry over spilled milk," "Don't be greedy or ungrateful," and "When it's gone, it's gone."*)

Examples of common idioms and messages to help you get started include:

- "Money doesn't grow on trees."
- "A penny saved is a penny earned."
- "Waste not, want not."

- "A fool and his money are soon parted."
- "The more you have, the less someone else can have."
- "To whom much is given, much is expected."
- "With great wealth comes great responsibility."
- "Money is the root of all evil." (NOTE: The ACTUAL quote is, "The love of money is the root of all evil." Remember, money itself is neutral and can be used for good or evil.)
- Asking for more is dangerous and bad.
- Don't be greedy or selfish or unappreciative.
- Be happy with what you have.
- "Don't cry over spilled milk."

RESOURCE

The "Money Messages" cards from www.2164.net are excellent for blended families and couples.

After you've gone through your childhoods, share with each other meaningful stories and memories you have from your adult lives about lessons learned and the values and approaches to money you see you were expressing in those circumstances.

These conversations require openness, caring, and deep listening. Do your best to not interrupt each other, and avoid jumping in with your own stories and memories until it is your turn. Keep breathing deeply and give each other the space and safety to share the memories fully and completely.

What Talking about Money and Values Reveals

This conversation about values will also allow you to learn even more about each other, and not necessarily in the way you might imagine. So often we think that communication is about the *words* we are saying. Research on non-verbal communication reveals that our tone of voice and our nonverbal behaviors (body language, facial expressions, etc.) communicate a lot more than the words we speak.[9] As a listener we are not only tracking what is being said, but we are also assessing if the speaker means what they say. And you would be wise to pay attention to your fiancé's nonverbal cues as he talks about what matters most to him. Be careful to stay in reality and to not dismiss any red flags or concerns that might arise during the conversation. Make a mental note about what you notice that might bring up further questions. You each may even want to have a pen and paper to jot down what you're hearing, as this is a great way to reflect back to your beloved that what you're understanding matters most to him, and he can be invited to do the same for you.

Some examples of things to pay attention to during the values conversation include:

- Does your partner have a ready excuse and tend to blame others or situations for why they went into debt?
- Is your partner highly critical of you or others who might not be as smart, frugal, or successful as they

are when it comes to financial decisions?

- As your partner is telling you how much they love to save, are they shaking their head or looking away?

And, remember, when communicating intentionally about money, you will learn more about yourself too! For instance, you may notice what your reactions and emotions are as you talk about money:

- Are you defensive and wary?
- Are you embarrassed by how you've been taken advantage of by trusting the wrong people?
- Do you become more controlling, rigid, or insistent?

As you pay attention and stay connected, you can deepen your bond and strengthen your foundation by naming what you **notice without judgement**. We recommend being curious and interested, and treat this as a valuable discovery process. One way to stay connected is to not be afraid of emotions.

Values Clarification Game

Once you feel you have covered the major areas about money (spending, saving, investing, charitable giving, budgeting, taxes, debt—good and bad,... etc.), then it's time to have some FUN! Look at your sticky notes (or index cards) and treat them like a word game. Work together to put them into groupings that seem to go together. See which values you have most in common -- where there are relatively equal numbers of both colors represented in one, two, or three of the groupings. As you read them aloud together, you may find that a particular word or phrase combines all of those messages into one value. Do that for all the piles that have a good mix of both your colors. This is exciting, this is where your values overlap; this is your base.

RESOURCE

Consider purchasing these cards to further clarify your shared values. https://www.theintentionaladvisor.com

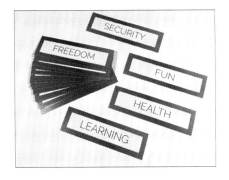

When Values Clash

For the groupings that are not well mixed—where you may have one value that means a lot to you and your partner has an opposing value that means a lot to him or her—you know that you have some important conversations ahead about what you will do when those two clash.

For example, Cindy M. loved to save and felt a sense of security in her life when her bank account had over $10,000 in it and her retirement contributions were maxed and matched. Her fiancé, Sam D., enjoyed working hard and gaining bonuses for a job well done. He liked to spend his rewards on things he wanted when he wanted them. He relished the freedom that came with receiving bonuses and found them to be a positive motivator when he knew he could spend freely and abundantly on items that helped him pursue his other interests, including hunting and fishing equipment, a new truck, and a trip to Africa. While Cindy's anxiety and irritation rose when Sam spent so freely, Sam had to fight feeling resentful or stifled when he saved for Cindy's needs and overrode his own desire to freely spend. The most important tip for couples facing these kinds of differences is to use the next essential ingredient . . .

2. Acknowledgment with Love and Courage

"But what I thought, and what I still think, and always will,
is that she saw me. Nobody else has ever seen me … like
that… Love is one thing — recognition is something else."
—Peter Beagle

Whenever we choose to share with each other our hopes, wishes, fears, histories, mistakes, failures, and humiliations about money, it is an act of love and courage. We are wired as human beings to immediately react to what is being told to us with agreement or disagreement. **This is not a conversation about agreement or disagreement; this is a conversation about building trust, awareness, and understanding of each other's points of views and perspectives.** The best way to

refrain from judging or drawing conclusions is to catch judgments when they start and shift to appreciating each other for choosing to share at all!

The roots of the word "courage" are wisdom and heart, and you want each of you to feel that you were wise in openly telling each other the truth about your views on, beliefs about, and experiences with money. And, you want to know you have chosen your life partner wisely and not just from your heart alone. Here are some approaches to loving acknowledgments for your consideration:

- Honestly acknowledge each other with heartfelt, authentic appreciation for this conversation.
- Appreciate that you are giving each other the opportunity to get to know each other even better.
- Be grateful that you are building your capacity to be safe enough to speak openly with each other about very intimate and difficult topics.
- Acknowledge how you are strengthening your

relationship as you discover where you are aligned AND where you are going to likely have conflict and disagreements.

This process, as we have seen repeatedly with couples who are committed to going the distance, will make it even safer to keep sharing *about anything* with each other.

Giving and Receiving
Loving Acknowledgments

For most people, it is much easier to give an acknowledgement than to receive one. As a couple, you want to build both these acknowledgment muscles together, as they will support you in navigating your prenup conversation the entire way through, and will serve your marriage for years to come.

There are a few specific ways to authentically acknowledge your partner that will be most meaningful and effective:

1. **Keep it specific and present**: "When you spoke about how your father treated you when you took money from his dresser drawer, I really appreciate your having shared how painful and challenging that was for you and the impact it had on your relationship with him."

2. **Keep it short and to the point**: "I appreciate that you really listened to me and that you were willing to do the values exercise with me."

3. **Keep it personal and meaningful to him or her**: "I want to acknowledge you for how hard you work and all of the ways you support us now and into the future."

While these are useful tips, the most important thing is to be authentic when you acknowledge each other. Don't say something you don't mean! This will go over like a lead balloon. And, if your partner's acknowledgment of you is hard for you to hear or believe, take a breath and have them say it again, then look them in the eye, breathe deeply, and see if you can feel it in your heart. This is a very useful and important exercise to do with each other every night. You'll be amazed by how connected you will feel and how you will be able to easily access your love and appreciation for one another throughout each day.

Red Flags

If you experience your partner holding his cards close to his vest and not being as open as you'd like, or, if he is saying things that contradict other things you've heard him say or seen him do, then you need to slow things down, now! These are indicators that there may be a breakdown in trust that needs to be addressed. Don't ignore these signs. You want to address them sooner rather than later. This brings us to the next essential ingredient: how to assess and create trust with each other.

3. Furthering Trust

"What I found was that the number one most important issue that came up to these couples was trust and betrayal. I started to see their conflicts like a fan opening up, and every region of the fan was a different area of trust.
'Can I trust you to...' ."
—John Gottman[10]

Trust is the core foundational element of a prenup conversation. Without it, you risk having what Patrick Lencioni, author of *The Five Dysfunctions of a Team*, calls "artificial harmony." When you are in "artificial harmony" with each other, much is left unsaid, and what you think you agree to in the conversation is not actually what one of you may want or need. When this occurs, the process will likely be derailed as you get closer to signing documents.

In order to build the kind of trust that will allow you to go the distance, you need to be able to be vulnerable with each other, and to be confident that your respective vulnerabilities will not be used against you. According to Lencioni, "the vulnerabilities I'm referring to include weaknesses, skill deficiencies, interpersonal shortcomings, mistakes and requests for help."

To better understand trust, you can learn more from Charles Feltman, the author of *The Thin Book of Trust*. He defines trust as choosing to risk making something you value vulnerable to another person's actions. He then breaks down the concept of trust into four assessments. Instead of merely labeling someone as untrustworthy, you can dig deeper and define which of the four assessments you are struggling with. The four assessments are:

- Sincerity
- Reliability
- Competence
- Care

When you understand that you both are always assessing whether you can trust each other, it is important to look at which area of trust you are focusing on. For example, when one of you promises to do something and you don't do it, the other will tend to think that you were insincere, when in fact, you may have totally meant to do it and are unreliable. Or maybe you feel incompetent to do it and are taking time to learn how to before attempting it, so that you can produce what your partner requested. In relationships we tend to quickly jump to the presumption of insincerity and we miss the chance to explore what might be keeping the promise from being fulfilled.

As a couple getting ready to talk about your prenup, you are most definitely assessing at each stage whether or not your beloved **cares about what you care about**—and when he disagrees with you, you will inevitably assess that he doesn't care—and this is a dangerous assessment to make and live in. With this framework, you will be much more empowered as a couple to slow things down, not jump too quickly to agreement or disagreement, and to not presume a lack of care, or a lack of trust, as you explore your different approaches and perspectives.

Let's face it, the moment the topic of a prenup comes up, the first thought is "What?! Don't you trust me?!" or "Why do we need a prenup when we love and trust each other?" As we have explored throughout this guide to starting your purposeful prenup, your **prenup conversations will do more to ground and deepen your trust** than anything else you talk about—if you approach it with intention.

Introducing These Ideas to your Fiancé

You know your beloved better than we do. With that in mind, we aren't going to tell you how exactly to approach him, but here are a few approaches we know to be successful (depending on how open he is and how "alpha male" he is) are:

1. The Ninja Approach: Instead of asking him to read this book, pull out some ideas and try them. Start with one thing you think he'll be most open to, and take baby steps.

2. The Aikido Approach: Have it be his idea. Be curious about how he wants to approach the conversation, and offer one of the ideas as something that might further HIS thinking.

3. The Straightforward Approach: Imagine simply reading this book together and getting going with your marriage right now.

The Future

"There is no more lovely, friendly, and charming relationship, communion or company than a good marriage."
—Martin Luther

When you take the time to make sure these ingredients of **Core Values**, **Loving Acknowledgments** and **Authentic Trust**, are measured, refined, and thoroughly mixed together, you are much more likely to have a smooth start to the prenup conversation. The most important thing is to connect on what you care about, and assure each other that you are taking into consideration what your beloved cares about as well! Keep a win–win attitude as much as you can.

Word of Caution

We would not recommend that you attempt to have a prenup conversation before you have established your shared values about money with each other, before you have developed an ability to easily give and receive acknowledgments from each other, and before you have established that you have sufficient trust in your capacity to have the conversation effectively.

If you are in a time crunch, hiring a professional to help you have the prenup conversation is your best bet. Contact us or find a collaborative lawyer or collaborative therapist in your state who can assist you in the dialogue and help you when it gets bumpy or difficult. Don't attempt to have it without support and without these foundational ingredients firmly in place, or those cracks will take hold and erode your foundation.

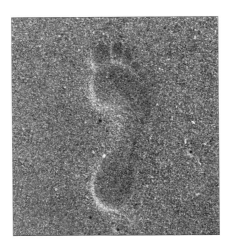

The Next Step on the Journey

This book was designed to help you dip your toe in the water and give you a chance to get started from the best position possible. We wanted to give you some great resources you can use as you begin to embark on your prenuptial-agreement journey. This is indeed a journey, so as you traverse it, think of us as trusted guides who have helped many couples successfully navigate some of the tricky spots on the river ahead. Let's link arms and stay connected so you can be successful each step of the way. Feel free to reach out to us to ask questions, and gain perspective and resources from others navigating these same challenging waters. We can learn from each other, guide each other, and keep each other from getting dashed on the rocks along the way.

RESOURCE

For updated information about Purposeful Prenups and other resources to strengthen your marriage, visit www.purposefulprenups.com

How We Help

Even with this guidance, the next step can be daunting. We're here for you. We marry the qualitative and quantitative sides of prenups, i.e., the relational and legal. On the relational side we offer coaching through the prenup process to do exactly what we've laid out in this book—strengthen your relationship during these important conversations. We can travel to you or use video conferencing. Our engagements are generally three sessions with ongoing support as needed.

On the legal side, we can represent you in negotiating and drafting your prenup or help you vet an attorney who can represent you from the place of purposefulness. If you have an attorney, we can consult and coach you as you work with your lawyer to ensure the process does not become adversarial in nature as they attempt to vigorously represent you.

We are also often brought in by other therapists, coaches, financial consultants and lawyers when the process stalls or worse. We're happy to bring purposeful prenups to people around the country.

For more information, visit www.purposefulprenups.com

Happy wedding, marriage, and peace of mind with your prenup!

About the Authors

Since 2004 Emily has worked with ultra-high-net-worth families on strengthening trust, improving communication, and preparing family members to take on roles and responsibilities in their family businesses, estate plans and philanthropic endeavors.

Emily Bouchard has facilitated over 130 family meetings spanning three generations where their net-worth ranged from $2m to $1.5b. She has also worked with over 100 affluent women on building their confidence and competence in their financial decision-making. She joined the Wealth Legacy Group in 2009 and became managing partner in 2010.

In 2015 Emily became the "family transitions" faculty member of the Exit Planning Institute. She works collaboratively with families and their advisors to support family members through some of the most challenging decisions and life events they will ever face. She presents, facilitates, and coaches women, couples, families, and groups on addressing the emotional issues related to life's transitions.

Since 2003, Emily has been considered a leading expert in the field of blended family dynamics. She has been featured in popular media, including The Today Show, CNN, WSJ, Bloomberg Businessweek and The New York Times. Emily co-authored, with L. Paul Hood Jr., *Estate Planning for the Blended Family*.

Emily earned a B.A. with honors in Child Development from the University of Pennsylvania, and a Masters Degree in Social Work from the University of Texas at Arlington. Wanting to better understand the repeated dynamics she witnessed again and again in families, she became certified as a Money Coach for individuals, couples and businesses in 2008 through the Money Coaching Institute.

Emily currently lives in the San Francisco Bay Area of Northern California.

Emily Chase Smith believes strongly in the mission of Wealth Legacy Group. As a twenty-year attorney she has seen firsthand how the breakdown in interpersonal relationships can lead to ludicrous legal actions. Cracks in the foundation happen long before attorneys are called in to resolve issues that could have been prevented at the outset.

Co-author of the forthcoming book *Purposeful Prenups*, Emily brings to her strong transactional background reviewing and drafting contracts, business buy/sell agreements, estate planning documents, leases, and releases. She takes her understanding of formation of business relationships and documents into the courtroom assisting clients with business litigation, mobile home related matters, quiet title and will contests.

Emily served as an Adjunct Professor for Kaplan University, Hope International University, and Anglo-American College in Prague teaching Legal Research, Legal Analysis and Writing, Legal Technology, Legal Terminology, Ethics,

Legal and Ethical Issues in Business, Real Property and Introduction to Law.

Emily is the author of *The Financially Savvy Entrepreneur; Navigate the Money Maze of Running a Business* published by Career Press and has ghostwritten over 20 books on legal, business, and leadership topics.

Emily lives in Dana Point, California, with her three children, puppy and a garage so full of surf and paddleboards she has to park outside.

How We Met

The auditorium was filled with money nerds. Over two thousand financial bloggers, podcasters, advisors, authors, bankers, and assorted hangers-on were gathered for the big opening event of FinCon 2016. Secure in her front-row seat, Emily Chase Smith strategized about how to get a picture with Clark Howard, the keynote speaker and icon on par with Brad Pitt in the financial world. This would assure her favored-child status with her mother, relegating her brother and sister to second tier forevermore, but fate had bigger things planned.

Taking the stage before Clark was Jean Chatzky of NBC's *TODAY Show.* Chatzky was on stage with money blogger Chelsea Fagan, recording a live version of her podcast, HerMoney.[11] As the interview progressed, Fagan made a comment about people who "had a lot of money they didn't

want to talk about . . . if you live in New York, you know a lot of people whose parents pay their rent and they're, like, thirty . . . they have a source of money they are clearly playing down . . . whatever it is, they don't like to talk about it, and if you talk about it, . . . they assume you're doing it because you're jealous, because you hate them, because you kind of want to put their business on Front Street . . . "

Smith listened, slightly distracted due to plotting how to secure the life-altering photograph, and wondered if Clark had bodyguards to prevent her from rushing the stage. The Chatzky–Fagan interview moved into money confessions from the audience, ranging from that of a landlord whose foray into real estate started with her own eviction to that of another whose Starbucks spending hit $1,000 a year. The last money confession came from Emily Bouchard.

Bouchard had been sitting much farther back in the audience, taking in the whole scene, as this was her first experience at FinCon. She felt a bit like a fish out of water, having only dabbled in blogging, and possessing a distinctly different clientele than 99 percent of the people there.

As the interview with Chatzky exposed Fagan's disdain for people who Fagan perceived had hidden wealth or financial support from family, Bouchard began to feel a spike of energy traveling up her spine. She wanted to address Fagan's comments head on, to defend her clients and to take care of the hearts and minds of the people in that audience who felt the sting of her overt animosity, but didn't know how to do so. That was until Chatzky asked the audience to share their "money confessions." Before she knew what was happening, Bouchard was standing at the microphone, her heart racing. Chatzky looked her over and said, "We have time for one more."

Bouchard began:

This is challenging, and exciting, and very apprehensive because Chelsea, you're so willing to be so outspoken. My money confession has to do with the privilege you spoke about. My name is Emily. I'm from Wealth Legacy Group, and I work with the 1 percent. I work with inheritors who deal with a lot of shame and guilt around the benefits they get.

And they have to deal with a lot of hostile envy, and micro (and even macro) aggression from the popular culture. And this is actually harming all of us because it causes "stealth wealth."

When I was in social-work school, I experienced this. I needed a car to drive to school—from Dallas to Arlington, Texas—and my stepmother, whose lease for her Lexus was up, offered buy it out and give it to me. I immediately told her, "No! I can't park a Lexus in the parking lot of the social-work school!" This was very evocative for me.

When I began attending social-work school, I didn't have any notion that I'd be working with the population I'm working with, and it has been an extraordinary experience to honor their journey as well, and to really look at, no matter how much we have, we all have our own issues with money, and this has given me more compassion in all my interactions.

Smith's ears perked up at hearing her own first name, and she was intrigued by Bouchard's money confession. Despite having worked for years as an attorney in financial-practice areas, writing *The Financially Savvy Entrepreneur,* and ghostwriting a dozen financial books, she had never considered this perspective on the wealthy. Could the life of the 1 percent be less than perfect? Bouchard's name was easy for Smith to remember, so one Emily reached out to the other via the FinCon app, and a lunch at the iconic Anthony's Fish Grotto on the San Diego shore was arranged.

As she waited for Bouchard in her car in front of the venue, Smith worried. An entire lunch with someone she didn't know—would the conversation hold up that long or would they be left staring into their respective bowls of clam chowder? She needn't have worried. They were kindred spirits connecting. Bouchard shared her work and vision for *Purposeful Prenups*, and almost spat out her chowder when Smith shared that, along with being a professional author, she was also a single mother and an attorney who was very interested in a book project on prenups that could actually strengthen relationships. Bouchard and Smith spent the rest of FinCon brainstorming, planning, and dreaming, and *Purposeful Prenups* was born.

Here's a photo of one icon who is all about saving money and a photo of two icons in the making who are all about saving marriages before they even start.

References

1. Holland, K. (2015, February 04). We know why you and your spouse will fight tonight. Retrieved October 19, 2017, from https://www.cnbc.com/2015/02/04/money-is-the-leading-cause-of-stress-in-relationships.html

2. Dean, G. (2014, April 25). For Love or for Money: Should You Get a Prenup? Retrieved October 18, 2017, from https://money.usnews.com/money/blogs/my-money/2014/04/25/for-love-or-for-money-should-you-get-a-prenup

3. Grant, K. B. (2015, January 20). Prenups: Not just for the 1 percent anymore. Retrieved October 19, 2017, from https://www.cnbc.com/2015/01/20/prenups-not-just-for-the-1-percent.html

4. J. (2009, July 16). #3: Steven Speilberg and Amy Irving: $100 million. Retrieved October 18, 2017, from http://www.zimbio.com/The+10+Most+Expensive+Celebrity+Divorces/articles/NB6jFu-KPsZ/3+Steven+Speilberg+Amy+Irving+100+million

5. Gaille, B. (2017, May 20). 19 Interesting Prenuptial Agreement Statistics. Retrieved October 18, 2017, from http://brandongaille.com/18-interesting-prenuptial-agreement- statistics/

6. Folk-Williams, J. (2012, April 21). John Gottman on Trust in Relationships - Storied Mind. Retrieved October 19, 2017, from https://www.storiedmind.com/relationship/john-gottman-trust-relationships/

7. https://www.gottman.com/about/research/couples/

8. Oxlade, A. (2013, May 23). Money habits are 'formed by age seven'. Retrieved October 19, 2017, from http://www.telegraph.co.uk/finance/personalfinance/10075722/Money-habits-are-formed-by-age-seven.html

9. B. (n.d.). HOW MUCH OF COMMUNICATION IS REALLY NONVERBAL? Retrieved October 19, 2017, from http://www.nonverbalgroup.com/2011/08/how-much-of-communication-is-really-nonverbal

10. Gottman, J. (2011, October 29). John Gottman on Trust and Betrayal. Retrieved October 19, 2017, from https://greatergood.berkeley.edu/article/item/john_gottman_on_trust_and_betrayal/

11. Episode 26: LIVE From FinCon, Where Money Nerds Unite. (n.d.). Retrieved October 19, 2017, from https://www.jeanchatzky.com/podcasts/episode-26-live-fincon-money-nerds-unite/

Resources

To Watch:

Video:

> "T'ain't what you do, it's the way you do it."
> https://www.youtube.com/watch?v=OVIWdrBDnxQ

Video:

> Kanye West: Golddigger
> https://www.youtube.com/watch?v=6vwNcNOTVzY

Video:

> Mashup: Seinfeld Scene and Kanye West
> https://www.youtube.com/watch?v=oALV78Ek6R0

To Read:

Book:

> *The Thin Book of Trust: An Essential Primer for Building Trust at Work,* by Charles Feltman

Made in the USA
Middletown, DE
19 January 2020

83416510R00033